The Crisis Opportunity

Henry A. Foster

DOD Publications

The Crisis Opportunity
Published by DOD Publications LLC.

Copyright © 2025 by Henry A. Foster.
All rights reserved.
Cover Design: Alexandria Stubblefield.
Cover Image: Grapix from Canva.

ISBN: 978-1-967603-00-8 (paperback)

Printed in the United States of America

DEDICATION

In memory of my parents, Mother Mattie B. Foster and Dad Ulysses Foster, Sr., who were instrumental in me staying true to my calling.

TABLE OF CONTENTS

ACKNOWLEDGMENT

I thank God for the ability to complete this work. All praise brings to Him! I especially thank Him for my wife and me being able to see this dream happen. She and I have long talked about writing books. This has been a shared vision for us. To jointly share in recognizing a widespread problem and then be given a joint solution to share with all who read our books is fantastic. It is terrific that here we are preparing the Word of God in book form - both playing a role - and giving those tools that they need to be successful and to receive the fullness of the blessings of God. For more than twenty-five years, this has genuinely been a teamwork effort.

I thank my wife, Apostle-Senior Pastor Wilma C. Foster, for standing and advancing the Kingdom of God with me. I am also thankful for Breakthrough Ministries and the members of whom God has blessed me with oversight. I am grateful for how they have stood down through the years. Their prayers and belief in me and the vision that God gave me have been invaluable. I salute them with all sincerity. Finally, I acknowledge and thank God for my family.

INTRODUCTION

When we consider the term opportunity, it can be described as something good that results in a good or beneficial outcome. It is essential to recognize that not all opportunities for us come as we expect them. Some opportunities, often the most transformative ones, are presented as uncomfortable experiences, which is the case when faced with crises.

Every day, people around the world face crises. These can be brief or prolonged but range from mild to extremely intense. Crises are times of trouble, pressure, and difficulty. There are times and seasons of discomfort and loss. However, it's important to remember that a crisis is not just a challenge but also a fertile ground for learning, realignment, and, most importantly, growth. It's a seed of potential waiting to be nurtured, a classroom where life's most profound lessons are taught. Throughout this book, we will use varying scriptures to echo this point. Let's use Ecclesiastes 3:1-8 as our starting point:

> *1 To every thing there is a season, and a time to every purpose under the heaven:*
>
> *2 A time to be born, and* **a time to die***; a time to plant, and* **a time to pluck up that which is planted;**
>
> *3* **A time to kill***, and a time to heal;* **a time to break down***, and a time to build up;*

*4 **A time to weep**, and a time to laugh; **a time to mourn**, and a time to dance;*

*5 **A time to cast away stones**, and a time to gather stones together; a time to embrace, and **a time to refrain from embracing**;*

*6 A time to get, and **a time to lose**; a time to keep, and **a time to cast away**;*

*7 **A time to rend**, and a time to sew; **a time to keep silence**, and a time to speak;*

*8 A time to love, and **a time to hate**; **a time of war**, and a time of peace.*

Ecclesiastes chapter three, verses one through eight, illustrates twenty-eight seasons, fourteen of which could be seen as seasons of crisis. These crises, far from random occurrences, are transformative seasons of trouble, pressure, discomfort, and loss. They are not just challenges but also opportunities for us to learn, be tested and develop, even in the face of intense difficulties. They are the catalysts for our spiritual maturity and rulership.

So, how can these fourteen crises be an opportunity? Most people would say that they can't be. And they are correct in that crises are not considered an opportunity. Instead, they are viewed as times of problems or intense challenges that few want to endure. However, it's crucial to remember that there are unique 'crisis opportunities in each crisis we face.'

In this book, we will focus on crises as opportunities that result in a beneficial outcome, which is glorifying God. Every crisis we face is an opportunity for transformation. For instance, you may recall a time when you were faced with a severe monetary crisis. It was a time of intense pressure and difficulty, but it was also a time of great learning and growth. In that season, you may recall learning to trust in God's provision and to be more disciplined in your spending. Crises are often used to develop or reveal our condition, but always under His guidance. It's a chance to learn, be disciplined, and become the person God has destined us to be. Oddly enough, He does not use only comfortable situations or experiences to teach and establish us God uses our crisis opportunities to teach, prove, and grow us.

Chapter 1

TO TEACH

Do you have a crisis in your life? Join me and others who have experienced crises. God wants you to know that a crisis can help you. It can be a real blessing to you. It can serve as a class for you and me. Every crisis opportunity is a teaching moment for growth and spiritual development. A crisis can then serve as a training tool for us to teach how to recognize and submit to God, as well as how to obtain and keep His blessings. This chapter will discuss some lessons that God wants us to learn from our crises.

Recognize & Submit

Crises are designed to instruct us and bring us to recognize God's sovereignty. We must remember that God is sovereign, and as we remember, we must see the importance of learning to recognize and submit to His sovereignty. Psalm 24:1-3 reminds us that:

> *¹ The earth is the Lord's, and the fulness thereof; the world, and they that dwell therein. ² For he hath founded it upon the seas, and established it upon the floods. ³ Who shall ascend into*

the hill of the Lord? or who shall stand in his holy place?

Everything in the heavens and earth were created by and for Him, created by His great power and authority. There is no other or higher authority or power than He. He knows the beginning from the end. There is no one else who is more supreme or holier than Him. No one else created the earth with their words. Moreover, even God said in Isaiah 46:9:

> *Remember the former things of old: for* **I am God, and there is none else; I am God, and there is none like me,**

God uses these crises to reveal to our hearts and open our eyes to recognize who He is and His awesome sovereignty. Through crises, we learn that God doesn't have to answer to anybody. God is the only someone that's sovereign. Through crises, we learn that God is sovereign and doesn't just rule but overrules. He over-answers prayer. He's more than enough. He doesn't just give you a cup and let your cup get full. He gives you a cup, lets your cup get full, and fills it till it's running over. He doesn't let you catch fish just until your net gets filled. He lets it break and fills it up till it breaks wide open. So, God doesn't just accidentally meet your needs.

God is the only somebody who can take Pharaoh and make him raise Moses as his family. Pharaoh grew Moses up in his house to lead the people of God from it. Pharaoh fed, raised him, and let him ride on a golden barge down the Nile River. Moses was taught in his house the wisdom of Egypt. Because of God's sovereignty, He ruled and overruled in this situation. He wanted the same man that Pharaoh raised to lead God's

5

people out of Egypt before him. Now, you tell me that God isn't awesome.

While believers say we recognize God as sovereign, do we really understand how to recognize His sovereignty? Let's first look at what it means to "recognize" God. Recognizing Him means that we acknowledge His existence and authority. In Hebrews 11:6, we are taught that when we come to God, we must first have faith because without *it is impossible to please him*. Thus, our faith is not meant to be just a belief but a powerful connection that empowers us to recognize His sovereignty. Next, we are told that:

> ...*for he that cometh to God must believe that he is, and that he is a rewarder of them that diligently seek him.*

So, when we recognize God, we must acknowledge His existence, sovereignty, and ability to govern and provide for us. What does this mean? We recognize Him as One, whom we have encountered via Jesus, His Only Begotten Son. We were *saved by grace through faith* (associated reference Ephesians 2:8) and reconciled back to Him. Only God had the power and authority to design the plan of salvation. We must identify Him as the Holy One who has supreme authority in our lives because of the finished work of Jesus Christ. We embrace Him as our Creator and the Source of everything – salvation, righteousness, peace, and joy. In chapter 46 of Isaiah, we read that God reminded His people - the house of Jacob and the remnant of the house of Israel - of His sovereignty because they had recognized and submitted to it. However, they drifted away from this place of recognition and submission.

Crises also catalyze deepening our relationship with God. Can we confidently say that we understand who God is in His sovereignty – His authority, power, and presence – and then submit to Him? If not, we need to learn and understand what it means to submit to His sovereignty. Moreover, when we think we have learned something, we must not stop and assume that learning it once is enough. Instead, we need to continue growing in recognition and submission because we know that our faith should move from one level of faith to the next. Our learning and understanding of God and His Word should grow from one level to the next. We need always to be in pursuit of Him and deepen our desire to be more pleasing to Him through our increased faith, submission, and obedience. One method God uses to deepen our relationship with Him and teach us about His sovereignty and submitting to Him is through crises.

Now, here is the big question: Who's on the Throne? Is it God or me? Is it God or you? Here is where it gets tough. After recognizing His sovereignty, what's happening next? After you identify and know that He is supreme and has all power and authority, who is the boss, you, or Him? The boss is the one who is the highest responsible authority in our lives. The boss will be the person who is allowed to govern our lives. That person is the one who defines and equips us for our purpose and future. So, who's going to be in charge? Is it God? Who's "will" is going to be done in your life? The will that should be done should be who created you and me. How does the created or creation tell the creator that it has a mind of its own and plans to lead itself? A better example is how the car reveals to its design engineer or manufacturer that it has a mind and intends to rule itself. This is an interesting thing to consider. Somebody must decide if we will recognize and submit to His sovereignty – Power, authority, and rulership. Or are you and I going to struggle and kick and fight all the rest of our lives to the grave?

God uses our crises oftentimes to tell us to submit. Yet, we're just fighting all the way. Unfortunately, some people finally reach the last mile and still haven't submitted. They are still struggling to let their own will be done instead of God's will. That's a tough one, right there, but God exposes us so that we will see where we're at and what's in our hearts. God has a fantastic way of doing it because what God does is God exposes us to delegated authority, for example, to find out if we really will submit. I know you want to look holy and tell me, "*Honey, I'm submitting to the Lord*," but are you and I submitting the way He wants, and sovereignty requires? If we are honest with ourselves, we still struggle with elevating our will above His will. Let's take a look at Exodus the 17th chapter, starting at verse one:

> *And all the congregation of the children of Israel journeyed from the wilderness of Sin, after their journeys, according to the commandment of the Lord, and pitched in Rephidim: and there was no water for the people to drink.*

Now that *according to the commandment of the Lord* is talking about according to the leading of the cloud and the pillar of fire. This is not talking about God talking to them. It's not talking about God saying, "*Hey, come on, let's go this way.*" It talks about the "*following of the cloud,*" and "*it was pitched in Rephidim.*" Now, wait. There was no water for the people to drink. You can only imagine now that the people will struggle here, which they did. They struggled against this seeming lack of water.

God guided the children of Israel out of Egypt and through the wilderness, showing them a mirror of their hearts and selves through their crises. The water situation was one such crisis opportunity. The children of Israel went three days without water. When they arrived at Mara, they found water but could not drink from it. They had water to drink, but it wasn't very pleasant. This meant the water had a sharp, unpleasant taste, which resulted in them experiencing disappointment. This crisis became an opportunity for them, and now for us to see a failure of expectation. This crisis opportunity was one of several sharp, bitter experiences that they experienced. This is a stark reminder of their struggle and God's testing of their submission problem, a test repeated throughout their journey. Let's continue on with verse two in the same chapter:

> ² *Wherefore the people did chide with Moses, and said, Give us water that we may drink.* **And Moses said unto them, Why chide ye with me? wherefore do ye tempt the Lord?**
> ³ *And the people thirsted there for water; and the people murmured against Moses, and said, Wherefore is this that thou hast brought us up out of Egypt, to kill us and our children and our cattle with thirst?*
> ⁴ *And Moses cried unto the Lord, saying, What shall I do unto this people? they be almost ready to stone me.*

So, Moses says, and I'm paraphrasing here, "*Wait a minute. Now, you aren't arguing with me. You're arguing with the Lord.*" Now, let me say this. This was about a one day's journey from where they were, according to what I read in the concordance, about one day's journey from where they were. They don't have any water. The last time they traveled, it was a three-day journey. Unfortunately, they are about to get mad again.

The children of Israel were something else when you think about this. If God hadn't kept the bread and water on the table for them, these people would have been a mess. I mean, God met every need they had. Yet, if God didn't constantly do everything instantly, these people weren't satisfied. That's how people get today if God doesn't continually move when they say move or do what they say to do. I tell you; God never answers prayer on our schedule. He isn't interested in our timetable. Since He knows the beginning from the end, he knows where the cliff's edge is. He is not concerned about how scared you and I are because we don't even know where the cliff's edge is. So, you are saying, *"Lord, don't let me fall over the cliff."* And God says, *"Well, don't you see the invisible shelf I got out there? You're not going to fall."* However, since you can't see it, we can't see it, we get afraid and don't trust God. We think we're about to fall over the cliff, but God doesn't get excited about it because God knows. Thus, God doesn't answer any prayer on our timetable. I want you to remember that as you pray and follow the Lord. That is essential.

God is not concerned about answering prayer on your timetable. Your timetable doesn't excite God. *"Answer me tonight, Lord."* God may wait two more days before answering our prayers. God may do you as He did Lazarus. *"So, you say that he's dead?"* Lazarus' being dead didn't bother God. It didn't bother Jesus. Lazarus, dead for three days, still experienced God's power and authority. So, you didn't get the money in the mail like you thought you would yesterday? *"Well, Lord, I told you I needed this money yesterday."* And God didn't get excited. You are excited. I am excited, but He's not excited. That old song is true that He may not come when you want Him, but He is right on time. Before you fall over the cliff, He will get you. And if He doesn't get you before you fall over, He could get in the air. And if He doesn't get you in the air, He can soften the ground. He will do something to help you, but He will always answer. We must know we can't wrestle against or press God to operate on our timetable. Let's return to our passage Exodus the 17th chapter:

> *²Wherefore the people did chide with Moses, and said, Give us water that we may drink. And Moses said unto them, Why chide ye with me? wherefore do ye tempt the Lord?*
>
> *³And* **the people thirsted there for water; and the people murmured against Moses**, *and said, Wherefore is this that thou hast brought us up out of Egypt, to kill us and our children and our cattle with thirst?*
>
> *⁴And Moses cried unto the Lord, saying, What shall I do unto this people? they be almost ready to stone me.*

The people thirsted for water, and the people murmured. They murmured against Moses. This is not their first time murmuring. Let me tell you what is interesting here is that the very thing that they continually accuse Moses of trying to kill is the only somebody – their children – who is going to make it to the promised land. They continued to murmur about how he was going to kill them and their children. Yet, the only ones who made it were their children. The people who didn't make it were those who murmured, complained, and didn't submit.

Welcome to your crisis opportunity, a kind of school of submission, to learn how to recognize and submit to God. It's a tough learning time. Are you submitted to the Lord? Resisting the Lord's rule over you will eventually lead to open rebellion. I don't care who you are or where you come from. I don't care how much you think you know about the Bible; if you continually refuse to submit and resist the rulership of God in your life, it will eventually lead to open rebellion against God. Then everybody will get the chance to see that you don't and will not submit to Him. Everybody knows what happens to a young man who continually breaks the law. A young man who is constantly resisting rulership and authority in society and won't pay attention to anybody, what happens to him? Does he eventually come to a place where everybody knows he's a resistor? He comes to a place where everybody in town can see that this guy doesn't care about law, authority, or anybody. Anyone who continually refuses to submit to the rulership of God, if they constantly do it, trust me, will eventually be exposed openly. Everybody will get a chance to see that they resist what God wants in their life. You and I should never want to be that way.

God will bless our tossing and turnings. By that, I mean sometimes, we wrestle and struggle. God will bless us even during and in times of our struggles. However, it's important to note that God will not bless open rebellion. *Rebellion is as the sin of witchcraft* (1 Samuel 15:13a). So, He definitely will not bless rebellion. God's response to our struggles and His response to rebellion are starkly different. He will bless you in your tossing and turnings, even when fighting to overcome sin. He can still bless you through that. This doesn't mean that He blesses your sin or celebrates your sinning. So, this does not give people a license to sin. God will, however, bless you in your crying out, humbly submitting yourself before Him and seeking His help to overcome the sin. However, if you rebel openly against God and His authority, this includes His delegated authority, He doesn't take that light at all. Rebellion is serious with God. Let's look at Isaiah 66, the first two verses:

> *¹Thus saith the Lord, the heaven is my throne, and the earth is my footstool: where is the house that ye build unto me? and where is the place of my rest?*
>
> *²For all those things hath mine hand made, and all those things have been, saith the Lord:* but **to this man will I look, even to him that is poor and of a contrite spirit, and trembleth at my word.**

Here, we learn about the kind of person that God regards, and that person recognizes His sovereignty, has a reverence for His Word, and humbles themselves. Thus, He is looking for people who submit to Him in recognition of and reverence for who He is and His sovereignty. If we were talking about you, we're talking about how people view and treat you, which means we respect you. Your answers and your opinions are well respected and believed and carry weight. However, imagine that it reaches another level when there is humility and submission in their heart when you speak. When this humility and submission in the heart occurs, you do not get them rising against what you're saying, but they are being submitted to it. And that's what God wants from His saints about Him, His sovereignty, and His delegated authority.

God wants submission and sends us to school through our crisis opportunity to see it. In our crisis, He lets us see how we will act. Some people fail the submission test over and over and over again. However, they pass the test of fasting, praying, and reading their Bible. They passed all those tests but failed the one for submission.

I almost hate to talk about submission sometimes because one of the first things people like to think about is that when a pastor talks about submission, he's talking about people needing to get under his shoes and shut up. However, that's not what this is about. We're talking about submitting to God and then submitting to God through delegated authority. That's one of the toughest things in the world. It tends to be especially tough for young people, ministers, and others. Yet, that's the kind of person God loves to honor, who is submitted to Him and His delegated authority.

Let's now take a look at a familiar scripture, James 4:6:

> *But he giveth more grace. Wherefore he saith, God resisteth the proud, but giveth grace unto the humble.*

What does it say? God gives *more grace* and *resists the proud* but gives *grace unto the humble*. Right at the end, He says, "*Submit yourself.*" So, He must be talking about submission. God gives grace to the humble. He gives them more grace. More grace means that sometimes you might need a little more grace. Many times, what people need is just a little more grace and a little longsuffering. God suffers a little longer with us. Grace is God's unmerited favor, and it's also God's ability to apply Christ's death to reconcile us from our sins. What a sovereign God that we serve. Let's be found guilty of recognizing and submitting to His sovereignty and will.

Obtain & Keep

Like with the children of Israel, God can use our crises to help us prepare to enter and keep the promised land. These crises could be financial difficulties, health issues, relationship problems, or any other situation that challenges our faith. These crises come to reveal some things about us and in our hearts. Without this revealing of our hearts, we make mistakes or refuse to do things God's way, putting our promises of God at risk of losing them. Most of us have had some stuff and have lost it. How many people have been blessed financially, and it seems like it has drifted away? You had money. Everything was going fine, and then, it started dwindling. God showed you the promise or promised land. God blessed you to get it, but you didn't have what it took to keep it. How many people know that there are people who've been healed before but that there was something that they didn't keep their healing? Crises can produce in us what it takes to obtain and then keep what God wants to give us. Lots of people have said, "*I have the victory.*" And then two weeks later, don't even ask them how they're doing because they have lost it somehow. One way that He can teach us how to get and keep what He has for us is by revealing our needed posture and weapons that we have to use.

God wants to teach us to stand and conduct ourselves in crises. He also wants us to learn to recognize and embrace the authority and power we received because of Christ Jesus. God wants us to be overcomers. These desires that He has for us contribute to the type of posture that we need to have. So, God puts us in situations where we encounter conflict, teaching us how to engage in spiritual warfare. Spiritual warfare is the battle in the spirit realm, where we take a stand against the forces of evil using our weapons. And we know that the "*weapons of our warfare are not carnal but mighty through God to the pulling down of strongholds"* (2 Corinthians 10:4). At the same time, some Believers don't want to have to do spiritual warfare but know that we're not going to ever outgrow spiritual warfare. You will never get so spiritual that you don't have spiritual warfare. You'll never get to where you become immersed in God so much that there is no conflict, spiritual battle, or warfare. You will never get to that point. You never will, so then we must adjust our minds and get our attitudes to where we know one thing we've got to do: we've got to fight. We've got to fight the good fight of faith and lay hold on learning that the Sovereign God is with us. He is not only with us but also the Source of everything we need to be victorious in every battle.

As our sovereign Source, He has given us weapons to help us in our crises. God wants us to learn how to overcome our battles and crises. We learn to use these weapons first by reading about them and being equipped by the Holy Spirit to use them, but only when we put them into practice do we walk in what He has given us. This journey of learning and growth is a testament to our spiritual development, inspiring us to continue our fight with renewed vigor and determination.

So, what has He given us that we get to learn how to apply during a crisis? During a crisis, we can grow in our prayer life for one. Our prayer may expand to include faith-filled confessions and confessions requesting God's help, such as *"Lord, teach my hands to war and my fingers to fight"* (reference Psalm 144:1). Other weapons that we get to exercise, learn how to use, and strengthen our use of include, but are not limited to, the Word of God, the name of Jesus, the Blood of Jesus, faith, and binding and loosing (see the Resources section of this book for some scriptural references). Becoming aware and skilled with our weaponry is essential. More importantly, yielding to and relying on the power of God through the person of the Holy Spirit is critical. We will never do anything for the Lord until we learn how to overcome in our battles.

Many of us don't understand what happens to us in battle. Many times, some people end up being battle-scarred and battle-worn. However, we must keep fighting, for the war is not over. I serve you notice that just because you win one battle doesn't mean the war is over. When we're not at war, we must be prepared for war, which means we always stay ready. Yet, that's why you have so many weak Christians who, many times, can't seem to fight one battle with the devil and win because they have never learned how to prepare for or overcome in battle. You don't prepare for battle when it's convenient. You remember what God's Word says about you, your authority and power, and weapons. Recognizing God's sovereignty and all that power on your side should cause you to have a different posture. You also don't overcome being weak. You must learn to be strong in the Lord and the power of his might. And nothing can be done without faith. Our strength, power, and victory come from Him.

One thing about it is the tempter, the devil, and the kingdom of darkness are forever trying their best to allure, to attack the people of God all the time. The ultimate goal is to destroy us. The devil looks, watches, and waits. His master weapon is deception. He always seeks a way to deceive us and destroy our faith and relationship with the Lord. He is always looking for an opening where he can destroy our faith and destroy our relationship with the Lord Jesus Christ. And he would like to destroy our productivity if he could do that. If he can't destroy your faith and can't destroy your relationship with the Lord, then he begins to attack in some other way. The devil, our spiritual enemy, is constantly seeking to undermine our faith and disrupt our relationship with God. He always has sneaky ways to destroy our productivity when we're unproductive, such as distracting us with worldly desires or causing us to doubt our abilities. He doesn't care as much about us being Christian and Kingdom people as he cares about making it so that we're not producing anything. We exhibit dominion when we are fruitful, multiply, replenish, and subdue. With that dominion, our God-given authority is manifested in every situation. Therefore, as good stewards, we can rule and reign in every crisis.

Chapter 2

TO PROVE

While crises serve as a learning tool or school to teach us, they also serve as a mirror, reflecting the actual condition of our hearts. Crises expose us to what is in our hearts. God, on the other hand, already knows what's in our hearts. He's the only one with access to understanding men's hearts. Men don't know their hearts, so He exposes your heart like a teacher who reveals the correct answers after a test. If you ask people, do you know your heart? Do you understand what's going on in there? Some might say yes. However, they would be wrong. They do not. How can we know the heart of men or our own?

Our ability to know ourselves is limited. Often, we don't see how we will respond to situations until they occur. We may think we will act one way only to discover later that our responses differed. That's why God has to expose our hearts so we will know what's in there. God indicates in His Word that He knows more about you and me than we do. Let's take a look at Exodus 16:4:

> *Then said the Lord unto Moses, Behold, I will rain bread from heaven for you; and the people shall go out and gather a certain rate every day,* ***that I may***

prove them, whether they will walk in my law, or no.

Amazingly, God will rain down bread from Heaven and use it to prove to the people whether they will walk in His law or not. You may ask yourself: "*how will bread coming from Heaven prove that you walk in God's law?*" This word, prove, could mean to test, reveal, or examine to show you who you are. Now, a crisis can serve as a time of training to indicate where you are and the condition of your heart and expose your intentions. This bread situation became a crisis opportunity to see what was in their hearts. It demonstrates whether they would be satisfied with God meeting their needs. Oftentimes, people struggle like the children of Israel. God meets our needs. The things that we try sometimes to fulfill ourselves don't work out. God shows us that there are needs that only He can meet. We all have tried to meet our needs or dictate/regulate how they should be met until we found out that only God can meet them. God can only fulfill our deep satisfaction and deep desire in our hearts. Did you know that the flesh can never be satisfied? You can never satisfy the flesh.

Reveal

Israel had many crises in their life, and the purpose of the crises was to reveal or manifest the condition of their heart. God exposes you and me to many things and puts us in many situations. This includes allowing us to come into challenging situations because God wants to reveal the contents of our hearts. What's in our hearts often exposes who is on the throne or whose will we are following chiefly, and many times, it surprises us. See, we don't know what's in our hearts. We may think that our hearts and motives are pure, but what does God see and say about the contents of our hearts? Does He agree with our assessment of ourselves? Or does He see something else? As the Bible says in Jeremiah 17:9:

> *"**The heart is wicked and deceitful above all.** And **who can know it?**"*

Don't we often look so good and smug, like our hearts are so pure? It should be, but do you know we don't know the contents of our hearts? It takes the Word of God, yielding to the Holy Spirit, and a crisis in our lives to expose the conditions of our hearts because we don't know what they are. You will never know what's in your heart sometimes until there is pressure put on you or a crisis. A man only shakes hands with himself when there's pressure or crisis. Other than that, he doesn't even know who he is himself. However, if you want to meet yourself, you must shake hands with yourself. I don't know about you, but I met myself, and I was not all I thought I was. Some people close their hands in the door and don't say bless you. Instead, they say something else, like a cussword, and then doubt or question whether they did when asked about it. It takes a crisis to expose our hearts. So, if we don't have any crises, we don't know what's in our hearts.

God allows us to have crisis opportunities to show us who we are. He already knows who we are, but we don't know. We often think we got it together. Peter, for example, thought he had it together in Mark 14:29-31:

> *[29] But Peter said unto him, although **all shall be offended, yet will not I.***
>
> *[30] And **Jesus saith unto him,** Verily I say unto thee, that **this day, even in this night, before the cock crow twice, thou shalt deny***

me thrice.

[31] *But he spake the more vehemently, If I should die with thee,* **I will not deny thee in any wise.** *Likewise, also said they all.*

Here, Peter is in a situation and is about to have a crisis opportunity. Again, I'm paraphrasing here. He said to Jesus, *"I'll never leave you. Not me, Jesus."* Yet, he was going to do it and do it a few times. He was going to deny Jesus before the cock crowed three times. He was being told, *"You're going to deny."* And he confidently replied with a *"no, not me…I'm going to die with you, baby."* And when the cock crows the third time, he had denied him three times. Jesus looked at him, and Peter just dropped his head and wept because he said, *"How did you know that was in me?"* Jesus says, *"I know more about you than you do."* That's what our Bible highlights for us.

Let's travel to the Old Testament and look at another example of God wanting to prove and reveal something to us. Look at Exodus 20:20, Deuteronomy 8:2, and Judges 2:22-23, where God tells us that he intends to prove to us to reveal something:

> *And Moses said unto the people, Fear not: for* **God is come to prove you,** *and that his fear may be before your faces, that ye sin not.* Exodus 20:20

> *And thou shalt remember all the way which* **the Lord thy God led thee these forty years in the wilderness, to humble thee, and to prove thee, to know what was in thine heart, whether thou wouldest keep his commandments, or no.** Deut. 8:2

*²²That through them **I may prove Israel, whether they will keep the way of the Lord to walk therein**, as their fathers did keep it, or not. ²³Therefore the Lord left those nations, without driving them out hastily; neither delivered he them into the hand of Joshua.* Judges 2:22-23:

The children of Israel in the wilderness are our model for us to look at when we are not really walking in all the ways God tells us to walk in. Most people are not walking in the ways the Lord told us to walk in. We can look at the children of Israel and see where they got off track. Furthermore, we can see where we are. Are we where we think we are, walking in His ways and keeping His commands? If we are unsure, know this: if we say that we are His, He will *"prove us"* to show us where we are. During the during, He may use crisis opportunities that involve things like conflict or disappointment.

Proving us is essential to God. In His sovereignty, He has the power, authority, and legal right to make known to us with evidence what truly exists in our hearts. As stated previously, crises are how God does this. Our crisis opportunities are a chance for Him to show us where we are or are not, and because of who He is, He gives us a chance to get it right. Isn't that awesome? God doesn't just expose the condition of our hearts for the sake of doing it. He doesn't do it so we can see and feel like failures and can't make it, but we should humble ourselves and submit ourselves so that a correction can occur.

Correct

As mentioned in other sections, God puts us in and exposes us to situations and things to show us what is in our hearts. Afterward, He corrects us. Correction is a word that doesn't excite people. Instead, it can cause people to cringe when it's heard. He can correct anybody. He can correct the Pope, the governor, the preacher, and the bishop. It doesn't matter. God will correct anybody. Let's be honest, and our flesh doesn't like correction. It doesn't easily submit to another's will, nor likes to do so, such as to God's Will. However, correction is crucial and beneficial to believers and their spiritual growth. How do we know? Well, I'm glad that you asked. Let's walk over to the Word of God in Hebrews chapter 12, starting at verse five:

> *5 And ye have forgotten the exhortation which speaketh unto you as unto children, my son,* **despise not thou the chastening of the Lord, nor faint when thou art rebuked of him:**
> *6 For* **whom the Lord loveth he chasteneth,** *and* **scourgeth every son whom he receiveth.**

Do you know that God loves you? From the verses we just read, we must see that correction is not rejection. Many times, we think correction is rejection. That's why often, if the preacher preaches and he says something, it hits you where it hurts, right? It hits you where that little sore spot is, and he puts the thumb on it and gets to twist it, which hurts. We believe that somebody's after us. We often get an attitude and take offense right away, but correction is not rejection. This is a good point to say to yourself that correction is not rejection.

Affirmations are essential, and here is one for you. Tell yourself that correction is not rejection and that God still loves you.

Let's continue reading in Hebrews chapter 12, verses seven and eight:

> *⁷If ye endure chastening,* **God dealeth with you as with sons;** *for what son is he whom the father chasteneth not?*
> *⁸But* **if ye be without chastisement,** *whereof all are partakers,* **then are ye bastards, and not sons.**

If we despise God for correcting us, God says we're not really His children. If we can't stand people chastising us, then what will happen? Now, we have to know that it is the Lord, of course, who is doing chastising. However, God sometimes allows people in your life to function as the chastiser, right? God disciplines us so that we will be sons. If we accept the chastisement of the Lord, then He says we are not bastards. Instead, we are sons of God. What does it mean to be a bastard here? It means if you reject the chastisement and nobody can straighten you out, then you become a bastard because you don't truly belong to Him. And eventually, you're going to leave God. Yet it's fantastic that we will allow people in life to correct us, but we don't expect the Lord to correct us.

It is essential to mention that God is not reaching out of the sky with a belt to chastise or correct us. He uses people and brings about situations – crises. And He said that if we allowed our unsaved parents, unholy people, or people who don't know the Lord, not only that, but people, even if they know the Lord in comparison to God, they're not sovereign and holy like Him. If we allow them to chastise us, I'm paraphrasing here, but He said, *"How much more should you allow God to chastise you."* God will never correct you for nothing. I might chastise people for nothing. Have you ever made a mistake, spanked your child, and found out later that the child was innocent? I have, but when I discovered the child didn't do it. I felt so bad. I couldn't believe that I whipped him for nothing, poor little old fellow.

As believers, we have to face the fact that many times, some of the things that we are talking about, we have to and should look at ourselves. Some of the things we've done. Then, when we look at a Holy God who never makes mistakes, never corrects you, or disciplines you unless there's a reason. If we allow people to correct us, to discipline us, and we allow it, and we grow up and thank them for it, how much more should we thank God that's true for his disciplining of us? Our posture should be more like, *"Lord, I'm so glad you wouldn't let me get away with that. I was on the wrong path. I was about to get over into something that was really, really messed up."* We should be thankful. I am so grateful that God didn't let me do some of the things I wanted to do.

Chapter 3

TO DEVELOP

In today's challenging times, God is not distant but ever-present. Furthermore, despite whatever crises we face, we must learn to see that good can come of them. These crises serve as a mirror, revealing our hearts and guiding us toward spiritual growth. God has several methods for developing His people. When He develops us, it can often look, feel, and be as though He is disciplining us. In these cases, we may think it is the devil but not the devil. It's God's way of educating us, and it's God Himself. The reason is that God is interested in character more than He is in your ministry, program, or anything else.

God had to guide me in a new direction. This new direction involved what His interests are. First, people often want to build a "house" for God, a big new building, or further develop existing ones. He wants us to have places of worship where His name can be in that place perpetually, but God is not that interested in a physical house or a physical building. While I am not saying that we can't build or grow our churches or support structures, I am saying that this is one thing that God is not as interested in building or developing as much as we are interested in it. Instead, God is more interested in building and developing us – we who are His temples. This is the house that

He is most interested in developing, bringing us together, and making us a spiritual house. That's what God is interested in more so than a big physical church building where the people are as cold as icicles. He has no interest in such cold places. His Spirit is not resident there and not moving among the people. He wants to build a spiritual house where we are lively stones that make up the spiritual house.

I also used to believe that God was more interested in my ministry than in developing my character. However, He clarified to me that He values character over ministry. He said, "*… I'm not so excited about the ministry I've given you.*" He said, "*But I want character because, without character, ministry doesn't mean nothing.*" And He told me, "*Stop rebuking the devil for everything that comes your way.*" I said, "*You're sure it's not the devil?*" He said, "*No, not this.*" He says, "*I've got to deal with you. That's what I have to do.*" I said, "*Well, praise the Lord.*" I know that this sounds comical, but at the time, it wasn't initially. Later, when I understood better what God was doing and its benefits, I was thankful. Similar to Paul, who shared this with the church in Philippi that (Philippians 4:12, AMP):

> *I know how to get along and live humbly [in difficult times], and I also know how to enjoy abundance and live in prosperity.*

He learned how to be content in whatever situation or crisis, knowing that the challenging times also benefited his growth. I, too, came to understand that crises, while challenging, are tools God uses to develop us. This understanding reassured me and instilled a sense of confidence. I grasped then that God wants to build our character and raise our awareness of

Himself and His abundant, ever-present resources, ensuring we always feel secure and supported.

Character

God's Word indicates that crises help to prove men's hearts by revealing our true character and the depth of our faith in Him. Let's go over to 1 Corinthians 10:

> *¹Moreover, brethren, I would not that ye should be ignorant, how that all our fathers were under the cloud, and all passed through the sea;*
>
> *² And were all baptized unto Moses in the cloud and in the sea;*
>
> *³ And did all eat the same spiritual meat;*
>
> *⁴ And did all drink the same spiritual drink: for they drank of that spiritual Rock that followed them: and that Rock was Christ.*
>
> *⁵ But **with many of them God was not well pleased: for they were overthrown in the wilderness.***

Wow. What is He talking about here? God was not well pleased with many of them, not just a few. Reading and seeing this passage is important because many folks sometimes say teaching or preaching the Old Testament is out of order for this age and this day. However, the Old Testament, the Bible tells us it's written for our examples. We can look at the Old Testament. See everything that you want to see that is not in the New Testament being acted out. Some of it, you have to go over into the Old Testament, see it, and then put it together with what is in the New Testament. Now, let's continue to read the remainder of the passage:

> *⁶Now **these things were our examples**, to the intent we should not lust after evil things, as they also lusted.*

I want to also look that this same passage in the Amplified Bible:

> *⁶Now **these things [the warnings and admonitions] took place as examples for us**, so that we would not crave evil things as they did.*

This lets us know that some of the things written about the children of Israel when they were in the wilderness. Additionally, it lets us know that everything in the Old Testament is for our example. In the same chapter, but verse eleven, He said:

> *¹¹Now these things happened to them as an example and warning [to us]; they were written for our instruction [to admonish and equip us], **upon whom the ends of the ages have come.***

So, the Lord desires a strong character in us. He uses crises to shape and develop us into what He envisions. Just as Israel faced numerous crises, we, too, will face multiple crisis opportunities. The purpose of these opportunities is to reveal the condition of our hearts and foster character development. God's plan is truly magnificent. Similarly, we encounter crisis opportunities to refine our character. This process is necessary because, as I've mentioned before, we are not fully aware of the contents of our hearts; only God is.

Our character is critical to our right now and our future. Our character can hinder what God wants to do through us. Your and my character speak to what kind of moral qualities we have. It talks about whether we can be trusted or not. I often ask folks: *"How far can your name take you or your children go with your name?"* Your name, the trustworthiness associated with it, benefits both you and your children, and children's children. And that trustworthiness is tied to your character. So, *how far can they go on your name?* Is your name associated with someone who can be trusted or who is deceitful or hateful? Are you known as a glory-stealer or one who credits God for what He has done?

Our character, yours, and mine, should be such that we leave a lasting legacy for our descendants. This legacy is based on our covenant with God through Jesus Christ and our trustworthiness in God's eyes. This is not an overnight transformation. God often has to revise our life stories to bring us to this point. In this process, He uses situations to add, remove, or both from our character and reputation.

In a crisis, let's not start blaming God and laying stuff on Him, making us no good. Just know that whatever God does with us, to us, through us, and for us, it is for our good. This includes discipline, which is a sign of His love. You and I will never be what God wants us to be if He doesn't deal with us. God loves us, so He is going to deal with us. His Word tells us that if He loves us, He will chastise us. Now, you notice God didn't say some sons, but He scourges every son He receives. There's been something where God had to let you know who He was. It was a little something that didn't feel so good, but He was developing your character. Developing our character puts us in a better position to learn and walk in the abundance of God's resources.

Awareness

In the prior section, your crisis opportunity has been seen as a learning tool or school to build your and my character. Let's look at crises as a school where your awareness is developed. So, what about our awareness that needs to be developed? One thing is an awareness of the abundance of God's resources. We sometimes forget that our God is sovereign and prosperous. He owns everything. There is no lack in Him. Sometimes, people look at their situations and lose sight of the fact that our God created everything but also owns everything. We say that *the Lord is our shepherd, and we shall not want* (associated reference Psalm 23:1), but do we believe that? Or are we just talking? Of course, we grow in our knowledge of God, and we should. So, we need to grow in our awareness and faith in His ability to provide for us and the abundance that He has accessible to Him. So, how rich is God? Let's take some time to read and meditate on Deuteronomy 8:16-17:

> *16 Who fed thee in the wilderness with manna, which thy fathers knew not, that he might humble thee, and that he might prove thee, to do thee good at thy latter end;*
>
> *17 And* **thou say in thine heart, My power and the might of mine hand hath gotten me this wealth.**

Wait. Please pause here and look at what verse seventeen is saying. This verse highlights how some people may attribute their wealth and success to themselves, a perspective that can lead to a sense of self-reliance. However, it's crucial to acknowledge that our achievements are not solely our own but a result of God's grace, provision, and guidance. This next verse helps us raise our awareness of His truth, enlighten us, and strengthen our spiritual connection, guiding us toward a deeper understanding of His sovereignty and role in our lives (Deuteronomy 8:18):

> *18 But **thou shalt remember the Lord thy God:** for **it is he that giveth thee power to get wealth,** that he may establish his covenant which he sware unto thy fathers, as it is this day.*

So, a crisis can also bring us to a point where we realize the abundance of our Father's resources. Is anybody having a crisis right now or knows anything about tough times? You may think you know how rich God is, but you don't. You might know about one type of riches, but God's riches span the globe and beyond. Think about the *prodigal son* (parable is found in Luke 15:11-32). He knew his Father was rich. That's why he went to him, and I'm paraphrasing here, and said, *"Give me my goods. I have to leave here. Could you give me my money? Could you give it to me? It's mine."* His father said, *"Sure."* But he knew his Father had more than that because when he got hungry, the prodigal son said to himself, *"I'm just down here eating with the pigs."* He started thinking about all the stuff that his Father had. *"I need to go back home. He feeds the servants better than I'm eating down here."* However, that's just one way of knowing the riches of his Father.

The prodigal son didn't know the riches of his Father's mercy. See, that had never been revealed. All of the money had been revealed to him. Yet, when he comes staggering back home, raggedy, and with clothes off of him after being with the pigs, a Jewish boy comes back home, and his Father looks up and sees him coming, runs to him, and puts his arms around him. Instead of saying, *"Take him out back there and let him get with the servants,"* he said, *"Look, kill the fatted calf, bring the robe, and take my ring..."* The prodigal son now learns something new about God's wealth and resources. Now, he discovered that his Father is not only rich financially, but his mercy endures forever.

God allows us to be in crises just so He can show us something sometimes, like His mercy and riches. You and I need to know how rich God is. We need to know just how rich He is. Israel has manifested the condition of their heart, and when it happened, they spanned the spectrum with faith. They had faith. They had little faith. Never do they have great faith. And sometimes that shows what's in our hearts. We have no faith. Sometimes, we have a little faith, and then you have those few who trust God in the face of anything, who have great faith. Although you don't have all the details, you still believe Him, and He says, *"great faith."* You have faith that's beyond reason. If faith is just with reason, it isn't too good. Faith has to go beyond reasoning.

Being taught, proven, and developed exposes what needs to be done but also helps increase our understanding of God's will. Crises are not roadblocks but learning tools and steppingstones to the promises God has in store for us. They are blessings in the clouds of difficulty, reassurance that God is always with us, guiding us through the storms and leading us to the brighter days ahead.

RESOURCES

Here are some common scriptures to support you through your crisis opportunities:

Sovereignty of God

Genesis 1:1 - In the beginning God created the heaven and the earth.

Psalm 115:3 - But our God is in the heavens: he hath done whatsoever he hath pleased.

Proverbs 19:21 - There are many devices in a man's heart; nevertheless the counsel of the Lord, that shall stand.

Psalm 103:19 - The Lord hath prepared his throne in the heavens; and his kingdom ruleth over all.

1 Chronicles 29:11-12 - [11] Thine, O Lord is the greatness, and the power, and the glory, and the victory, and the majesty: for all that is in the heaven and in the earth is thine; thine is the kingdom, O Lord, and thou art exalted as head above all. [12] Both riches and honour come of thee, and thou reignest over all; and in thine hand is power and might; and in thine hand it is to make great, and to give strength unto all.

Psalm 135:6 - Whatsoever the Lord pleased, that did he in heaven, and in earth, in the seas, and all deep places.

Proverbs 21:1 - The king's heart is in the hand of the Lord, as the rivers of water: he turneth it whithersoever he will.

Isaiah 46:10 - Declaring the end from the beginning, and from ancient times the things that are not yet done, saying, My counsel shall stand, and I will do all my pleasure:

Matthew 19:26 - But Jesus beheld them, and said unto them, with men this is impossible; but with God all things are possible.

Proverbs 16:4 - The Lord hath made all things for himself: yea, even the wicked for the day of evil.

Colossians 1:16 - For by him were all things created, that are in heaven, and that are in earth, visible and invisible, whether they be thrones, or dominions, or principalities, or powers: all things were created by him, and for him:

Jeremiah 32:27 - Behold, I am the Lord, the God of all flesh: is there any thing too hard for me?

Isaiah 14:27 - For the Lord of hosts hath purposed, and who shall disannul it? and his hand is stretched out, and who shall turn it back?

Ephesians 2:10 - For we are his workmanship, created in Christ Jesus unto good works, which God hath before ordained that we should walk in them.

Jeremiah 32:17 - Ah Lord God! behold, thou hast made the heaven and the earth by thy great power and stretched out arm, and there is nothing too hard for thee:

1 Chronicles 29:11 - Thine, O Lord is the greatness, and the power, and the glory, and the victory, and the majesty: for all that is in the heaven and in the earth is thine; thine is the kingdom, O Lord, and thou art exalted as head above all.

John 1:3-4 - ³ All things were made by him; and without him was not any thing made that was made. ⁴ In him was life; and the life was the light of men.

Revelation 15:3 - And they sing the song of Moses the servant of God, and the song of the Lamb, saying, Great and marvellous are thy works, Lord God Almighty; just and true are thy ways, thou King of saints.

Psalm 104:24 - O Lord, how manifold are thy works! in wisdom hast thou made them all: the earth is full of thy riches.

Hope

Jeremiah 29:11 - For I know the thoughts that I think toward you, saith the Lord, thoughts of peace, and not of evil, to give you an expected end.

Isaiah 40:31 - But they that wait upon the Lord shall renew their strength; they shall mount up with wings as eagles; they shall run, and not be weary; and they shall walk, and not faint.

Romans 5:3-4 - And not only so, but we glory in tribulations also: knowing that tribulation worketh patience; And patience, experience; and experience, hope.

Psalm 119:114 - Thou art my hiding place and my shield: I hope in thy word.

Micah 7:7 - Therefore I will look unto the Lord; I will wait for the God of my salvation: my God will hear me.

Psalm 62:5 - My soul, wait thou only upon God; for my expectation is from him.

Spiritual Weapons:
Faith

Matthew 17:20 - And Jesus said unto them, Because of your unbelief: for verily I say unto you, If ye have faith as a grain of mustard seed, ye shall say unto this mountain, Remove hence to yonder place; and it shall remove; and nothing shall be impossible unto you.

Hebrews 11:6 - But without faith it is impossible to please him: for he, that cometh to God must believe that he is, and that he is a rewarder of them that diligently seek him.

The Name of Jesus

Philippians 2:9-10 - [9]Wherefore God also hath highly exalted him, and given him a name which is above every name: [10]That at the name of Jesus every knee should bow, of things in heaven, and things in earth, and things under the earth;

The Crisis Opportunity

1 Peter 3:22 - Who is gone into heaven, and is on the right hand of God; angels and authorities and powers being made subject unto him.

The Blood of Jesus

Exodus 12:23 - For the Lord will pass through to smite the Egyptians; and when he seeth the blood upon the lintel, and on the two side posts, the Lord will pass over the door, and will not suffer the destroyer to come in unto your houses to smite you.

Matthew 26:28 - For this is my blood of the new testament, which is shed for many for the remission of sins.

Revelation 12:11 - And they overcame him by the blood of the Lamb, and by the word of their testimony; and they loved not their lives unto the death.

The Word of God

Isaiah 55:11 - So shall my word be that goeth forth out of my mouth: it shall not return unto me void, but it shall accomplish that which I please, and it shall prosper in the thing whereto I sent it.

2 Timothy 3:16 - All scripture is given by inspiration of God, and is profitable for doctrine, for reproof, for correction, for instruction in righteousness:

Hebrews 4:12 - For the word of God is quick, and powerful, and sharper than any two-edged sword, piercing even to the dividing asunder of soul and spirit, and of the joints and marrow, and is a discerner of the thoughts and intents of the heart.

Armor of God

Ephesians 6:9-11 - [9] And, ye masters, do the same things unto them, forbearing threatening: knowing that your Master also is in heaven; neither is there respect of persons with him. [10] Finally, my brethren, be strong in the Lord, and in the power of his might. [11] Put on the whole armour of God, that ye may be able to stand against the wiles of the devil.

Prayer

Romans 8:26 - Likewise the Spirit also helpeth our infirmities: for we know not what we should pray for as we ought: but the Spirit itself maketh intercession for us with groanings which cannot be uttered.

Philippians 4:6-7 - [6] Be careful for nothing; but in every thing by prayer and supplication with thanksgiving let your requests be made known unto God. [7] And the peace of God, which passeth all understanding, shall keep your hearts and minds through Christ Jesus.

1 John 5:14-15 - [14] And this is the confidence that we have in him, that, if we ask any thing according to his will, he heareth us: [15] And if we know that he hear us, whatsoever we ask, we know that we have the petitions that we desired of him.

AFTERWORD

Every crisis we face is a divine opportunity for transformation. As we humble ourselves under the mighty hand of God, He begins His work—exposing, correcting, shaping, molding, and refining us like clay in His hands, like the Potter He is. In our submission and surrender to His will, He crafts something new in us and develops our character. No more kicking, fighting, or clawing to escape the pressure of the process—only trust in the One who knows the masterpiece He is creating and shaping.

When His work is complete, He does not leave us hidden. In His perfect timing, He exalts us, lifting us as a testimony of His love, grace, great power, and commitment to us. What was once a struggle becomes a display of His sovereignty and glory, a witness for all to see what God has done.

Yet, in our seasons of crisis, we must guard our hearts. Disappointment, unmet needs, and hardship must not turn into murmuring, doubt, or faithlessness. No matter how bitter the crises may seem, God's resources are abundant—His grace, wisdom, and love can sweeten even the most difficult circumstances.

So let us yield to Him. Let us embrace the journey, trusting that every hardship, challenge, and refining fire prepares us for something greater. In the hands of the Master, no crisis is wasted. We are being shaped, strengthened, and positioned so that in due season, His glory will be revealed in and through us.

Let the Lord shape you. Let Him make you. And when the time comes, stand as His work, a living testimony of His goodness.

Prayer of Submission and Trust

Lord, today I humbly submit myself to You. I commit my ways into Your hands, trusting that You will bring all things to pass according to Your perfect will. I am who You say I am. I receive what You have promised, and I walk in the strength of Christ, knowing that through Him, I can do all things.

I choose to be a believer, not a doubter—an active doer of Your Word, not just a hearer. Your truth transforms me, and I hide it in my heart so I may walk in obedience and honor You in all I do and say. As I acknowledge You in every step, I trust that You will guide my path, ordering my steps for Your glory.

Shape, mold, and make me into the vessel You desire so that in due time, Your work in me may be revealed and exalted for all to see. Let my life be a testimony of Your faithfulness. In Jesus' name, amen.

ABOUT THE AUTHOR

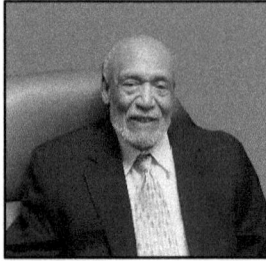

Henry A. Foster is the trailblazing Founding Apostle of Breakthrough Ministries, Inc. Anointed by the Lord, he teaches and preaches with a powerful prophetic fervor while operating boldly in the gifts of the Spirit. For more than fifty years, his ministry has illuminated the Word of God and transformed hearts across the United States. A devoted husband, father, and grandfather, Apostle Foster continues to lead with grace from his home state of Kansas alongside his wife.

Reaching, teaching, and inspiring people of
ages to see their greatness and fulfil their given
life's purpose.

The
Crisis
Opportunity

Henry A. Foster

---

www.ingramcontent.com/pod-product-compliance
Lightning Source LLC
Chambersburg PA
CBHW060809110426
42739CB00032BA/3161